I0202261

FORGIVENESS

Unless otherwise indicated, all Scripture quotations are taken from the Holy Bible: New International Version®. NIV®. Copyright © 1973, 1978, 1984, by the International Bible Society. Used by permission of Zondervan Publishing House. The "NIV" and "New International Version" trademarks are registered in the United States Patent and Trademark office by International Bible Society.

Verses marked NASB are taken from the New American Standard Bible®, © 1960, 1962, 1963, 1968, 1971, 1973, 1975, 1977 by The Lockman Foundation. Used by permission.

Verses marked KJV are taken from the King James Version of the Bible.

Verses marked ESV are taken from the English Standard Version.

Forgiveness: A 30 Day Devotional

ISBN 10: 1-931899-45-2

ISBN 13: 978-1-931899-45-1

Copyright © Basic Gospel 2020

Published by Basic Gospel

All rights reserved. No part of this publication may be reproduced, stored in a retrieval system, or transmitted in any form or by any means—electronic, mechanical, digital, photocopy, recording, or any other part—except for brief quotations in printed reviews, without the prior permission of the publisher.

Introduction

On the *Basic Gospel* radio broadcast, we talk about all kinds of life issues, but none more than forgiveness of sins. Year in and year out, forgiveness ranks as the number one issue our listeners are most concerned about.

I understand why. As the Bible declares, *"all have sinned and fall short of the glory of God"* (Romans 3:23). Each time we sin, questions about forgiveness race through our minds. We know Christ died on our behalf, but we are not sure what this means to us on a personal level.

Based on 30-plus years of ministry experience, I've come to these observations.

- All Christians know that Christ died to forgive their sins.

- Even with the clear declaration of God's Word that our sins have been forgiven through the finished work of Jesus Christ, Christians still struggle with fear and guilt. They wonder whether they've been forgiven.

- Confusion on this most fundamental truth hampers every other aspect of the Christian life.

Let me ask you. Do you know that God has forgiven your sins? Do you know you are a forgiven person in Christ?

The Gospel proclaims that you can know and experience God's forgiveness. What you are looking for is found in Christ's finished work on the cross. If you want to grow in your relationship with Jesus Christ and experience his love, the cross is the place to start.

For the next thirty days, let's take a fresh look at the finished work of Jesus Christ. As we do let's trust the power of the cross to lift the guilt and shame from our shoulders, turn our fear into confident faith and give rest to our souls.

At the end, I pray that we all know that we know that God loves us and that in Christ <u>we have</u> forgiveness of sins.

"To grow in your relationship with Jesus Christ and experience his love, the cross is the place to start."

Day 1

Hear it

For I delivered to you as of first importance what I also received: that Christ died for our sins in accordance with the Scriptures…(1 Corinthians 15:3 ESV).

Believe it

What are we supposed to do when we sin?

We ask this question because we all commit sins of every kind.

We tell lies. We covet our neighbor's stuff. We gossip. We steal.

We know we stand guilty. We know what we did deserves punishment and that the case against us is rock solid.

This raises that all important question. What do we do next? How should we respond after committing one of these sins?

This is an important question…one of the most important ones to our way of thinking.

But what if it's not the most important question?

What if there is a more important question we should be asking…one that is of first importance?

Well, there is and it is this: *What did Christ do for that sin?*

And that's where the Gospel, the good news, begins.

We want to know what we should do when we sin.

The good news does not start with us. Christ Jesus is the story. It is his work that is of first importance…that matters.

Here is what He did. Jesus Christ died for your sins.

He died for all the sins you've committed and for all the sins you will ever commit.

What needed to be done for your sins has already been done. Jesus became sin for you, so that you might become the righteousness of God in Him.

This is of first importance to God. This is of first importance to you.

Live it

Jesus died for your sins. All of them. Instead of punishment, he gave you mercy and forgiveness.

Is there a sin you've committed that you are wondering what to do about? Today, will you recognize that Jesus died for that sin? Will you, by faith, say thank you?

Day 2

Hear it

Without the shedding of blood, there is no forgiveness of sins (Hebrews 9:22 ESV).

Believe it

Why did Jesus have to die? He is the Son of God. He has all authority on earth and in heaven. Yet, he died a cruel and excruciating death. Why?

The answer is found in Hebrews 9:22.

"Without the shedding of blood, there is no forgiveness of sins."

This verse answers the why of the cross. If Christ had not shed His blood, there would be no forgiveness of sins.

But Jesus did die. He did shed his blood. In his blood is the forgiveness of sins.

What can we take from this? First, God desires to forgive. He doesn't want you to face the judgment and the penalty your sins deserve.

Second, Christ carried out the desire of his Father. Consider these words, *"Then I said, 'Behold, I have come to do your will, O God, as it is written of me in the scroll of the book'"* (Hebrews 10:7 *ESV*).

Jesus died to do the will of his Father. He shed His blood to forgive your sins. There was no other way.

And he is not going to die again. Consider this question: *"If you needed more forgiveness, what would Christ have to do?"* Is he going to die again?

Here is the good news – the blood Jesus shed one time was sufficient to take away all of your sins. Forgiveness is yours.

Live it

Remember, Christ shed his blood for you. This means your sins – all of them, past, present and future – are forgiven. The cross of Christ is the way of forgiveness. Commit Hebrews 9:22 to memory, note it in your Bible, and rest in this powerful truth.

Day 3

Hear it

But God demonstrates his own love for us in this: While we were still sinners, Christ died for us (Romans 5:8 ESV).

Believe it

Does God love you? Yes He does! Why is this most fundamental truth so hard for us to fully accept? God has made it very plain in the Bible, yet we're not quite sure the words apply to us.

I know. I lived many years wondering each day when God's punishment would come my way. It was a daily walk on spiritual eggshells. I knew He loved the world. I just didn't know that He actually loved me. How could he? I was always coming up short on what I thought were his expectations.

My constant failures kept me from seeing the love of God. Maybe you've had the same experience. Here's what it did to me. I had no assurance whatsoever. I lived in fear of God's punishment, felt guilty most of the time, and was plagued by constant guilt.

But it was my own legalistic thinking that kept me from truly knowing that God loved me. God reached out to me in grace. Unfortunately, I responded for many years through law rather than faith. Here's the good news.

God doesn't love us because we perform well. He loves us because he chooses to. And nothing we can do will ever change his choice.

He demonstrated that choice to love you through Christ's death on the cross. Knowing he did this for me while I was still a sinner changed my legalistic thinking. It was not my performance that mattered. It was Christ's. And with that, I could finally see clearly that God genuinely loved me.

Live it

To truly know that God loves you, look to the cross, not your performance. When you do, you can let go of that performance based Christianity, and walk confidently in the truth that nothing will separate you from the love of God.

Day 4

Hear it

In this is love, not that we have loved God but that he loved us and sent his Son to be the propitiation for our sins (1 John 4:10 ESV).

Believe it

Have you ever thought this about God: "No matter what I do, God is never satisfied with me."

The Bible tells a different story. God is satisfied. The biblical word is propitiation. It's not a word we hear very often, but it packs a powerful punch when it comes to our relationship with Jesus Christ.

Here is what we need to know. Propitiation is a God thing. It took place between God the Father and Jesus the Son. The writer of Hebrews marks it as a heavenly transaction: *"For Christ did not enter a man-made sanctuary that was only a copy of the true one; he entered heaven itself, now to appear for us in God's presence"* (Hebrews 9:24).

The end result is this: Jesus' shed blood satisfied the demands of God's justice and holiness. Think about that. God accepted the blood of Jesus as complete and final payment for your sins.

This is grace. Jesus accomplished for you what you could not accomplish yourself. This means there is nothing for you to do except believe. You will know you have truly believed when you are satisfied in your heart with Christ's death as total and complete payment for your sins.

This is *"by grace through faith."*

Live it

God is satisfied with the sacrifice of Jesus Christ on your behalf. Since God is satisfied with the payment for your sins, why shouldn't you be satisfied? Ask God to make this truth real in your heart and mind. God is satisfied. You can rest.

Day 5

Hear it

When you were dead in your sins and in the uncircumcision of your flesh, God made you alive with Christ. He forgave us all of our sins… (Colossians 2:13).

Believe it

Jim had a problem. One particular sin kept him in bondage and he couldn't shake it. Most of the time he was fairly certain God had forgiven his sins… at least 95%. But that 5% of doubt…at times it would keep him up at night.

Maybe that's the case for you. Your prayers are like a broken record. "Lord I did it again. Please forgive me, and I promise I will do better tomorrow." That's the way it was with Jim. He prayed. He read his Bible. He went to church. He promised God he would do better and try harder, but he never felt forgiven.

As a result, Jim's five percent of uncertainty started occupying one hundred percent of his thinking. The security and assurance he once knew gave way to fear and anxiety.

Jim's story is not unique. His doubts and fears are shared by Christians everywhere. We know Christ died on our behalf, but we are not sure what this means to us on a personal level. As a result, we live in fear of God's punishment.

A life filled with confusion and doubts and fear is not God's plan for you. He wants to clear away these negative emotions in your life.

If you want to know what God thinks about you, the cross is the place to start. As Paul said, he forgave all of your sins. Not some of them…all of them.

The place to start to solve the 95/5 problem is the cross. That all important question – *"Has God forgiven my sin?"* – is answered in the death of Jesus Christ.

Live it

Identify where you stand concerning the forgiveness of your sins.

Do you know that all of your sins have been forgiven? Or, are you 95% sure, 80% sure or 50% sure your sins have been forgiven? If you have doubts, are you willing today to take a fresh look at Christ's finished work on the cross?

Read Colossians 2:13 again and insert your name every place it says your, you, or all. The truth that all your sins have been forgiven will turn your doubt into assurance.

Day 6

🦻 Hear it

When he had received the drink, Jesus said, "It is fin-
ished." With that, he bowed his head and gave up his
spirit (John 19:30).

🧠 Believe it

It is finished! This was the last statement Jesus made
before he died.

But it was far more than just a statement; this was a
victory cry. The sin issue between God and man was and
is over. Jesus delivered the fatal blow to sin by taking it
away once and for all. What this means is that He paid the
debt, your debt, in full.

Because Jesus finished the work, forgiveness is now
yours. You stand before God as righteous, holy and ac-
ceptable in his sight.

Why is this truth so hard for us to believe? Why do we
struggle with the fact that nothing more needs to be
done, or can be done, concerning forgiveness of sins?

For me, I bought into the idea that it was my job to defeat
sin, to keep it out of my daily life. All I worried about was
how to keep from sinning, and then when I did, how to
get the black mark erased from beside my name. But the
black marks kept adding up and pretty soon, I wondered
if I was even saved.

I had this Christianity thing all wrong. I was trying to do
something Christ had already accomplished. He defeated

sin at the cross, and he forgave me of all my sins. His work was enough. He finished the task! I wasn't responding to Jesus's victorious cry through faith.

The good news is this: It is finished! The work has been done. Maybe it's time to simply believe that it's true.

Live it

Just three simple words comprise the most powerful, life-changing phrase in the entire Bible. *"It is finished."* Is it finished in your life? Do you know that in Christ you are a forgiven person? If not, let Jesus' victory cry become yours today.

Day 7

Hear it

How much more, then, will the blood of Christ, who through the eternal Spirit offered himself unblemished to God, cleanse our consciences from acts that lead to death, so that we may serve the living God! (Hebrews 9:14).

Believe it

A major cause of depression is guilt and shame. Many experience anxiety and depression because of things they did in their past. They are scared to death of the ramifications, like rejection from the people they love or punishment from God and others. They live burdened down by guilt and shame with the expectation of having to pay a heavy price for that thing they did in the past. That's why their future looks so bleak.

Here is the problem. They don't know what to do with their guilt and shame. They don't know how to break free. So they walk through life feeling, as one of my friends says, dirty and distant from everyone that matters to them, including God. Their consciences have never been cleansed.

There is a way to let go of guilt and shame, to live with a clean conscience. It is through faith in the shed blood of Jesus Christ. Consider this powerful passage from Hebrews 9:11-14:

"But when Christ came as high priest of the good things that are now already here, he went through the greater and more perfect tabernacle that is not made with human

hands, that is to say, is not a part of this creation. He did not enter by means of the blood of goats and calves; but he entered the Most Holy Place once for all by his own blood, thus obtaining eternal redemption. The blood of goats and bulls and the ashes of a heifer sprinkled on those who are ceremonially unclean sanctify them so that they are outwardly clean. How much more, then, will the blood of Christ, who through the eternal Spirit offered himself unblemished to God, cleanse our consciences from acts that lead to death, so that we may serve the living God!"

Jesus shed his blood once for all sin. He took away all sins forever, including yours. He dealt with them all. His demonstration of love cleanses the conscience. No longer do we have to hide or shrink back from God because we fear punishment. Jesus' shed blood invites us to draw near in full assurance of faith.

The cross of Jesus is the cure for guilt and shame. It is the truth that frees us from the sins of the past and enables us to walk in the freedom of God's love and grace today. Rejoice, you have been cleansed by the blood of the Lamb!

Live it

If you feel burdened by guilt and shame, know this: Jesus has already dealt with your sin. And as Paul wrote, God does not count your sin against you. Let this truth cleanse you once and for all and lift that guilt and shame off your shoulders. Rest today in Jesus' finished work, and walk confidently knowing that God remembers your sins no more.

Day 8

Hear it

In the case of a will, it is necessary to prove the death of the one who made it, because a will is in force only when somebody has died; it never takes effect while the one who made it is living (Hebrews 9:16, 17).

Believe it

Legally, a will is a statement of a person's wishes concerning the disposal of his property after death. When my dad died, everything he owned passed to Mom. That was his desire, and he explicitly expressed it in his will.

God has a will like that. It's called the New Covenant. In this will, God expressed his desires for you and me.

Before it could take effect, the one who made it had to die. *"In the case of a will, it is necessary to prove the death of the one who made it, because a will is in force only when somebody has died; it never takes effect while the one who made it is living"* (Hebrews 9:16, 17).

When Jesus gathered his disciples for the last supper, he raised a cup and said, *"This cup is the New Covenant in my blood, which is poured out for you"* (Luke 22:20).

The next day, Jesus died. He cried out in victory, *"It is finished."* The old had gone, the new had come. The long-awaited New Covenant was now in full force. When did the New Covenant begin? At the cross. Jesus' death changed everything.

This New Covenant is a covenant of grace. It is not like the Old Covenant, which was more like a contract between two parties. It was an *"if...then"* covenant. It included conditions for its fulfillment, but there are no conditions in the New Covenant. God promises, God fulfills.

As wills go, the New Covenant is not very long-only four provisions.

- *"This is the covenant I will establish with the people of Israel after that time, declares the Lord.*

- *I will put my laws in their minds and write them on their hearts. I will be their God, and they will be my people.*

- *No longer will they teach their neighbor, or say to one another, "Know the Lord," because they will all know me, from the least of them to the greatest,*

- *for I will forgive their wickedness and will remember their sins no more"* (Hebrews 8:10-12).

Live it

Don't underestimate the far reach of these promises where your life in Christ is concerned. These contain everything you need for life and godliness. In this New Covenant, you can live life to the full, because your sins have been forgiven and God remembers them no more.

Day 9

🦻 Hear it

For it is impossible for the blood of bulls and goats to take away sins (Hebrews 10:4).

🧠 Believe it

Every year, on the Day of Atonement, the high priest offered the blood of a bull and a goat for the sins of the people. They carried out their duties year after year because it was prescribed by the Law.

Even so, those sacrifices fell short. They covered the sins of the people, but they did not take the sins away. *"Otherwise"*, as the writer of Hebrews stated, *"would they not have ceased to be offered, since the worshipers, having once been cleansed, would no longer have any consciousness of sins"* (Hebrews 10:2).

Those sacrifices never cleansed the consciences of the people. Nor did they provide true forgiveness. The definition of the word forgiveness explains why. The Greek word is *aphiemi*. According to The Complete Word Study Dictionary, its primary meaning is *"to send forth, or away."*

True forgiveness comes through the sacrifice of Jesus Christ. He is the *"Lamb of God who takes away the sin of the world"* (John 1:29 *ESV*).

The blood of bulls and goats merely shadowed what was to come in Christ. Every year, those sacrifices served to remind the people of their sins…to recognize that the sin debt had not been paid in full…to show them they had not been made perfect.

But all that changed two thousand years ago. Jesus offered himself. He shed his blood. He took away your sins, all of them, once and forever. Through that sacrifice, he perfected you forever (Hebrews 10:14). Which means you can say with full confidence that your sins have been forgiven.

Live it

What does God do when he forgives sins? He takes them away once and for all. Rejoice! Through the shed blood of Jesus Christ, God sent your sins away forever.

Day 10

Hear it

…then he added, "Behold, I have come to do your will." He does away with the first in order to establish the second. And by that will we have been sanctified through the offering of the body of Jesus Christ once for all (Hebrews 10:9,10 ESV).

Believe it

God is holy…set apart…sanctified.

His appeal to the people of Israel was this: *"You shall be holy, for I the Lord your God am holy"* (Leviticus 19:2 *ESV*). That's a tall order if it is left up to us to make ourselves holy.

But it's necessary if we want a relationship with God. As the writer of Hebrews stated; *"without holiness no one will see the Lord"* (Hebrews 12:14).

The point is that holiness and unholiness don't mix. You and I fit into the unholy category. And if we were going to be in relationship with holy God, the changing had to be on our end. That's the problem.

Thankfully, this is not a problem for God. He has the power to make us holy…to set us apart for himself. And according to Hebrews 10:9, this is his will for you and me.

Jesus Christ carried out God's will through his death on the cross. He did away with the first covenant to establish the New Covenant.

It was that first covenant, the law, that gave us the knowledge of sin (Romans 3:20)…that showed us how far we missed the mark when it comes to holiness.

At the cross, Jesus established the New Covenant…the covenant in which God remembers your sins no more. Your sins have been taken away forever…forgiven once and for all in Christ.

Jesus' blood also set you apart…made you holy…so that you can know God and enjoy his love and grace forever.

What you could not do for yourself, God did through the shed blood of Jesus.

You have been made holy.

Live it

You may not feel like you are holy. And sometimes you will not act holy. The truth, however, is that you are holy. You've been sanctified by the blood of Jesus Christ. Let this truth soak in. It is the confidence you need to grow in your relationship with Jesus Christ.

Day 11

Hear it

He is the radiance of the glory of God and the exact imprint of his nature, and he upholds the universe by the word of his power. After making purification for sins, he sat down at the right hand of the Majesty on high (Hebrews 1:3 ESV).

Believe it

Recently an interesting video circulated on social media. The producers created a job listing for a director of operations and posted it online. Then they interviewed a number of applicants by video. For the applicants, the job description was beyond belief. First, it required the person to work 24 hours a day, 365 days a year. The person must be mobile and able to stand for long periods of time. No breaks. No vacation or sick leave. One applicant asked if it was legal to demand so much in a job. Another described it as inhumane. Several applicants asked about the pay. The answer came back, *"There is no pay."*

To this, every single applicant asked, *"Who would do such a job?"*

The interviewer assured them that literally billions of people currently occupy this position. Then came the punch line. *"They're called moms."*

The message hit home. These applicants gained an even deeper love and respect for their moms. It's true, you know–a mom's work is never done.

The same was true of the Old Testament priests. Their work was never done. The writer of Hebrews tells us what it was like for the priests. *"Day after day every priest stands and performs his religious duties: again and again he offers the same sacrifices, which can never take away sins"* (Hebrews 10:11). How would you like to be born into that bloodline? You stand to do a job day after day, again and again, and you never accomplish your purpose. You do that until you turn 50, and then the next generation steps in to carry on the work. Such was the fate of the priests.

But not Jesus. *"...when this priest had offered for all time one sacrifice for sins, he sat down at the right hand of God"* (Hebrews 10:12). The message is clear and strong. Jesus sat down because his work was finished. Jesus sat down because his blood satisfied the justice of God. He sat down because propitiation was accomplished. Concerning the sin issue, there is no need for Jesus to get up from his seated position.

Live it

In light of Christ's finished work, pull up a chair, take a seat and enjoy your place of rest in the finished work of Jesus Christ

Day 12

Hear it

Their sins and lawless acts, I will remember no more. And where these have been forgiven, there is no longer any sacrifice for sins (Hebrews 10:17, 18).

Believe it

"Bob," Lee said, "I'm calling to tell you that Basic Gospel changed my life. I was a very bad guy, I mean a very, very bad guy. But now I know my sins have been totally forgiven."

I admit, at first I wondered what in the world he could have done that was so bad. Whatever it was, the guilt of it trapped him in a dark place he thought he would never escape.

He had tried anything and everything he could to ease the pain and to somehow find peace. But nothing took away the enormous burden he carried. He thought he had out-sinned the grace of God and that there was no hope for him. But everything changed when he heard the message of Jesus' finished work on the cross.

He told me when the forgiveness of God hit his heart; he stopped his truck and screamed at the top of his lungs. I would have liked to have seen this big moment in Lee's life!

As Lee learned, we can't out-sin the grace of God. There is no line that we can cross that puts us out of God's reach. Jesus's blood has taken away all of our sins. As believers, we stand before him as forgiven people.

Live it

Even though you may remember your sins, God remembers them no more. Jesus' blood was big enough to take them all away. And because he offered himself, no other sacrifice for your sin is necessary. Your sins have been forgiven. That's news worth shouting from the roof tops.

Day 13

Hear it

For Christ died for sins once for all, the righteous for the unrighteous, to bring you to God (1 Peter 3:18).

Believe it

What is the question kids ask the most?

If you are a parent, you know the answer. It's *"Why?"*

It's a great question to ask. You can learn much about life when you are curious about the *"why."* I'm not sure we ask it enough when it comes to the Gospel.

For example, why did Christ die? We know that he did, but why? What did he have in his mind as the end result?

I like what Peter wrote in his first letter: *"For Christ died for sins once for all, the righteous for the unrighteous, to bring you to God"* (1 Peter 3:18). Why did Christ die? He died to bring you to God.

God created man for relationship. When sin entered in, that relationship was broken. Our fear of God's punishment kept us at a distance from Him. We were too afraid to get close. Jesus changed all that through His shed blood. It beckons us to draw near to God.

The writer of Hebrews put it this way: *"Therefore, brothers, since we have confidence to enter the Most Holy Place by the blood of Jesus…let us draw near to God…"* (Hebrews 10:19-22).

Live it

There is nothing to fear or worry about. Your sins are gone. Your punishment has been taken away. There is nothing standing in the way. Because your sins have been forgiven, you can *"approach God with confidence and freedom"* (Ephesians 3:12). This is good news.

Draw near and enjoy your relationship with Jesus Christ.

Day 14

Hear it

For God was pleased to have all his fullness dwell in him, and through him to reconcile to himself all things, whether things on earth or things in heaven, by making peace through his blood, shed on the cross (Colossians 1:19, 20).

Believe it

The Bible teacher somehow knew exactly what was going on inside of me. As if he was speaking only to me, he pinpointed the source of my frustration–trying harder, doing better and being better.

It's a path that doesn't lead to godliness, or to joy or peace.

I was living proof. The harder I tried to be God's guy, the more I sinned. The more I sinned, the more I tried harder to be good. It was a vicious circle which left me exhausted and frustrated.

I was frustrated because I couldn't figure out how the Christian life was supposed to work. *"Trying harder"* wasn't the answer. At that time in my life, Colossians 1:21 described my inner turmoil to a tee: *"Once you were alienated from God and were enemies in your minds because of your evil behavior."*

That is where *"trying harder"* leaves us–feeling like we are God's enemy. But that is not true. Christ's death on the cross shows the real story of God's heart toward us. As Paul wrote, *"But now he has reconciled you by Christ's physical body through death to present you holy in his sight, without blemish and free from accusation— if you continue in your faith, established and firm, and do not move from the hope held out in the gospel"* (Colossians 1:22, 23).

As my Bible teacher pointed out, I was holy in God's sight, without blemish and free from accusation. I didn't feel that way then, but that was and is the truth. Christ's reconciling work on the cross made it so.

I was trying to make it so by *"trying harder."* Here is a shocking truth. The phrase "try harder" is not in the Bible. You can't find it anywhere. What you do find is faith. The Christian life is lived by faith in Jesus. It is all about trusting the One who loved you and gave himself for you. Faith in Jesus is the simple route to victorious living.

Once I started resting in the love of God and took my focus off of my behavior, I began to experience freedom and joy as never before.

Live it

Maybe you believe God is telling you to try harder or be better. If so, will you let go of that thought right now? It did not come from God. He's already done the necessary work in Christ. You have been reconciled to God by the blood of Jesus. You are holy in his sight, without blemish and free from accusation. Now that's good news.

Day 15

Hear it

All the prophets testify about him that everyone who believes in him receives forgiveness of sins through his name (Acts 10:43).

Believe it

Consider the Apostle Peter. He denied the Lord three times. And after the rooster crowed the third time, Peter was undone. The Bible tells us, *"He wept bitterly."*

After the resurrection, Jesus did something for Peter that no one in Peter's shoes would expect. He lifted Peter out of his despair and counted him worthy to feed his sheep. That's grace.

Peter never dreamed this would take him into the Gentile world. Yet, God summoned him to the town of Caesarea to preach the good news to Cornelius, the Roman centurion, and his household.

For Peter, the mere act of entering Cornelius' house was a violation of Jewish law. An act that would defile him. But Peter entered anyway. Why? Because he had learned that God is not partial, that his love and life are available to all. That means you and me.

Peter opened his mouth and told this family about God's purposes for them in Christ. He concluded his message with these powerful words: *"All the prophets testify about him that everyone who believes in him receives forgiveness of sins through his name"* (Acts 10:43).

As he did, the Holy Spirit came upon these people. Forgiveness and life were theirs as the prophets had testified.

Here is the good news for you. The moment you believed in Jesus, you too received forgiveness of sins. Not for some sins, but for all of your sins.

Forgiveness isn't something God doles out to you with each sin you commit. No, he gave you this gift in full. You have forgiveness. It is yours "through his name."

Live it

Sometimes doubt fills our minds when it comes to forgiveness of sins. We are fairly sure God has forgiven our past sins, but what about the ones we commit today, and the ones we will commit tomorrow? What do we need to do to have those forgiven?

The message is clear. They have already been forgiven through the blood of Jesus Christ. And you already have his forgiveness for every sin–past, present and future. You received this gift of grace the day you believed.

Let this truth cast out all of the doubts. You are a forgiven person, fully alive in Jesus Christ.

Hear it

*In him we have redemption through his blood, the for-
giveness of sins, in accordance with the riches of God's
grace that he lavished on us (Ephesians 1:7, 8).*

Believe it

In my seventh-grade year, I belonged to a group of boys
who took on shoplifting as a challenge. One of the things
we would steal was the breath freshener, Binaca. Drug-
stores and convenience stores displayed it right next
to the checkout counter, making it a worthy challenge.
Could we get away with it? We did, or at least I thought
we did.

My friend, David, confessed to all our antics when confronted by his mom. And, of course, his mom called my
mom. She confronted me with one word, *"Binaca"*. That
one word shut me up. I couldn't deny my sin.

Fear gripped my heart. I knew punishment was close at
hand. I certainly didn't want to be punished, but I knew I
deserved to be.

My parents put my punishment in the hands of the store
managers. My dad took me to every store that I had
stolen something from and made me confess my crime
to the store manager. Fortunately, the managers were
lenient and only required me to pay for the items I had
stolen. But making restitution didn't ease my sense of
guilt.

What was God going to do to me? In my mind, God had to do something to me because sin can't go unpunished. I wondered if there was anything I could do to erase that black mark of sin and get back into God's good graces.

Out of fear, I pleaded with God for forgiveness and promised I would do better. I repeated the same process over and over again, but I never felt forgiven. This was my formula for forgiveness. The problem was that my formula didn't ease the guilt or take away the fear.

Ultimately, it left me wondering if I was even saved.

So I added to the formula. Confess, repent, ask God for forgiveness…and ask him to come back into my life. I probably asked Christ to come into my life more than 500 times. It was like my heart was a revolving door.

Live it

Christianity cannot be reduced to a formula. Every time I sinned, I relied on my faithful execution of the formula to move God to forgive me and assure me that I was saved. I was trying to earn something that had already been given to me by grace. When I believed on Jesus' name, I received the gift of forgiveness. God placed me in Christ, and in him, redemption, the forgiveness of sins was and is mine.

He did the same for you the moment you believed. Rejoice. You are in Christ. Which means, you have redemption, the forgiveness of sins. All in accordance with the riches of God's grace.

Day 17

Hear it

For he has rescued us from the dominion of darkness and brought us into the kingdom of the Son he loves, in whom we have redemption, the forgiveness of sins (Colossians 1:13, 14).

Believe it

I admire courageous souls who risk their lives to rescue others from oppression and enslavement.

Oskar Schindler did that during WWII and saved the lives of more than 1000 Jews during the Holocaust.

My friend Wally is doing it today rescuing and restoring the lives of young girls and boys from human trafficking.

Just recently, I watched a human chain form in the flood waters of Houston to rescue a pregnant woman from her home.

These are examples of people who respond to calls of help with no regard to their own safety. Heroic efforts like these inspire me because they reflect the story of God's great rescue mission.

Paul penned it this way: *"For he has rescued us from the dominion of darkness and brought us into the kingdom of the Son he loves, in whom we have redemption, the forgiveness of sins"* (Colossians 1:13, 14).

We were held in the powers of sin and death as lost people. We were dead spiritually. God put in place a rescue plan to save us.

Because of Jesus' death burial and resurrection, you are free.

God rescued you from the powers of sin and death and set you free to experience new life in Christ. And that's a rescue story worth sharing.

Live it

At a moment in time, God rescued you from sin and death through the death, burial and resurrection of Christ Jesus. He made you alive in Christ and sent the Holy Spirit as the guarantee of your rescue. And in Him, you have redemption, the forgiveness of sins.

There's no greater rescue than that.

Day 18

Hear it

Therefore, since we have been justified by faith, we have peace with God through our Lord Jesus Christ (Romans 5:1 ESV).

Believe it

Through Christ's act of propitiation, God showed us that he is just. He dealt with our sin. He didn't ignore it or sweep it under some heavenly carpet. He judged it, he condemned it, and he punished it. All obligations were fully satisfied. But that was not the end goal.

God is both just and the justifier. He freely justifies *"the one who has faith in Jesus"* (Romans 3:26 *ESV*). That's you.

Not only did God take away your sins, he declared you to be righteous. This is the proof that your sins have been forgiven and that God is fully satisfied with you. This means you are in right standing with God. You didn't work your way to that status. God justified you freely by his grace.

How does this play out in daily living? We still sin, don't we? And each sin we commit still deserves punishment. The punishment we deserve is death.

Yet, God says to those who are in Christ, "Your sins have been forgiven." How do we know that punishment is not waiting for us sometime in the future? What is the proof?

Justification!

God justifies sinners and declares them right in his sight on the basis of Christ's finished work on the cross.

The work is done. Jesus wants us to trust and depend on Him. It's in that trust that we can watch him work all things together for our good. We can trust him because he satisfied the law on our behalf. His punishment was our punishment. In exchange, His righteousness became our righteousness.

Live it

Through faith in Jesus Christ you have been justified... declared righteous. This is proof that all of your sins have been forgiven. Let this truth bring peace to your soul.

Day 19

Hear it

God made him who had no sin to be sin for us, so that in him we might become the righteousness of God (2 Corinthians 5:21).

Believe it

Have you ever heard someone say *"I need to get right with God"* or *"you need to get right with God"*? These statements are filled with fear and dread aren't they?

Here's an amazing fact. If you are a believer in Jesus, you are, and always will be, right with God.

Because of Jesus' finished work on the cross on your behalf, your sins and unrighteousness were exchanged for the righteousness of God.

Wow.

Jesus made you that way. This was his gift. Freely given by grace. Listen to Paul's words, *"God made him who had no sin—that's Jesus—to be sin for you, so that in him you might become the righteousness of God"* (2 Corinthians 5:21).

Through faith in Jesus, you have been made the righteousness of God.

Which means you are right with him now, tomorrow, next week, and eternally.

Because of Jesus' death, burial and resurrection, you will always and forever be right in God's sight.

Live it

Your status will never change. So take your stand on this truth. Rejoice that you have been made right with God.

And you will see the fruits of his righteousness transform your life.

Hear it

There remains, then, a Sabbath-rest for the people of God; for anyone who enters God's rest also rests from his own work, just as God did from his (Hebrews 4:9, 10 NIV).

Believe it

Jesus Christ finished his work.

He did everything necessary to take away your sins once and for all. Jesus put it this way in his high priestly prayer: *"I have brought you glory on earth by completing the work you gave me to do. And now, Father, glorify me in your presence with the glory I had with you before the world began"* (John 17:4, 5).

God the Father answered Jesus' prayer. He exalted him to the highest place – the right hand of the Father. He is seated there now.

What does this mean for you?

First, there is nothing more to do concerning your sins. Jesus has done it all. The fact that Jesus is seated at the right hand of his Father is proof.

The writer of Hebrews didn't want his readers to miss this point. For example, when comparing Jesus to the Levites, he explained that Jesus *"has no need, like those high priests, to offer sacrifices daily, first for his own sins and then for those of the people, since he did this once for all when he offered up himself"* (Hebrews 7:27 ESV). There is no need for Jesus to get up from his seated position.

This means you can rest. You don't have to *"try harder"* to earn God's love and forgiveness. No more begging or pleading for what you already have in Christ. The work has been done.

It's time to find your place of rest in the finished work of Jesus Christ.

Here is Jesus' promise to all who come to Him: *"Come to me, all you who are weary and burdened, and I will give you rest. Take my yoke upon you and learn from me, for I am gentle and humble in heart, and you will find rest for your souls"* (Matthew 11:28, 29).

Live it

Are you weary and burdened? That's not God's desire for you. He wants you to rest. You can because Jesus has already done the work.

Your sins are forgiven. You are righteous in God's sight. He loves you and accepts you. Believe it and take a rest in Him. It's time.

Hear it

When Jesus saw their faith, he said to the paralyzed man, "Son, your sins are forgiven" (Mark 2:5).

Believe it

Mark records a fascinating story in his Gospel account. A group of people were gathered at a house in Capernaum to hear Jesus preach the Word of God. The house was packed wall to wall with no room for another person.

After Jesus started preaching, four men arrived carrying their paralytic friend on a stretcher. They had heard about Jesus and his healing touch. This was their opportunity to help their friend. They were determined to find a way to get their friend into that house. The only option they saw was through the roof. They climbed atop the roof, cut an opening and then lowered their friend on his stretcher.

This was faith in action. When Jesus saw it, he looked at the paralytic and said, "Son, your sins are forgiven."

Does Jesus' response seem strange to you? His statement confused the crowd as well and certainly raised the eyebrows of the teachers of the law.

They were thinking, *"Why does this fellow talk like that? He's blaspheming! Who can forgive sins but God alone?"* (Mark 2:7). These teachers of the law packed deep theological truth in that seven word question. They clearly understood that forgiveness originates with God. God, and no one else, has the power and authority to forgive sins.

God is the offended party, the person that we ultimately wrong. Our sins are against him. Therefore, we are in his debt.

Jesus addressed their issue before they ever uttered a word. *"Why do you question these things in your hearts?"* (Mark 2:8 *ESV*). Then Jesus pressed his point. *"...the Son of Man has authority on earth to forgive sins."* Jesus, God in human flesh, with authority and power, forgave the paralytic.

What is fascinating is the paralytic's silence. He didn't say a word. He didn't ask Jesus to heal him and he certainly didn't ask Jesus for forgiveness. In fact, he wouldn't have even been there except for the heroic efforts of his friends. And, yet, Jesus delivered mercy with four simple words, "Your sins are forgiven."

Live it

Jesus says the same four words to you – *"your sins are forgiven"*. Do you truly believe that Jesus has the authority and power to forgive your sins? Do you truly believe that Jesus has forgiven your sins once and for all? If so, thank him right now for the forgiveness you have in Jesus.

🜨 **Hear it**

But whoever does not have them is nearsighted and blind, forgetting that they have been cleansed from their past sins (2 Peter 1:9).

🜨 **Believe it**

Nearsighted and blind.

It's a spiritual condition many believers suffer with today.

They can't see the good news of Jesus Christ because they are too busy focusing on their sin and guilt, their weaknesses and struggles, and their fears and frustrations. And it blinds them to their forgiveness in Christ.

The worst part is that it grinds their spiritual growth to a screeching halt.

Maybe you feel this way – like your spiritual growth has come to a screeching halt.

There is a simple reason. Peter identified the cause this way—you have forgotten that you have been cleansed from your past sins. Forgetting this truth puts fear, and specifically your fear of punishment, in charge of your relationship with God. And fear will keep you from "adding to your faith."

If you want to grow in grace, start with Christ's finished work on the cross. Resting in the truth that you have been cleansed gives rise to a dynamic and growing faith in Christ. Peter described it this way:

"For this very reason, make every effort to add to your faith goodness; and to goodness, knowledge; and to knowledge, self-control; and to self-control, perseverance; and to perseverance, godliness; and to godliness, mutual affection; and to mutual affection, love. For if you possess these qualities in increasing measure, they will keep you from being ineffective and unproductive in your knowledge of our Lord Jesus Christ" (2 Peter 1:5-8).

Knowing that you are clean, that your sins have been forgiven, is the key to your growth and transformation in Jesus Christ.

Live it

If you are not 100% sure that your sins are forgiven, today take a fresh look at the cross and thank God that he forgave you for all of your sins and cleansed you of all unrighteousness.

This will give you the eyes to see all that you have in Jesus.

Day 23

Hear it

Love keeps no records of wrongs (1 Corinthians 13:5).

Believe it

"Remember 5 years ago when you did…"

"And then, 3 years ago, you hurt my feelings when you said…"

"Even last Tuesday at 10:00 a.m., you…"

When it comes to our relationships with others, most of us keep a tally of the all the wrongs we have suffered. We have a list of all the wrongs our mates have done, one for our children, our employer, and our friends.

All it takes is one wrong word, and out comes "the list." We remind the person of their past sins against us and we hold these wrongs against them.

Many times, we feel that's how God interacts with us. As long as we're behaving properly, he loves us. But, if we mess up, out comes the list of all our past sins.

At least that is what we think God does. Based on that faulty thinking, the fear of punishment creeps back in and so does the guilt and shame.

But God isn't like that at all. Paul made this clear in his definition of love. He wrote that *"God keeps no records of our wrongs"* (1 Corinthians 13:5).

God does not remember your sins. He nailed them all to the cross, where Jesus' blood washed them away. Because of Christ's sacrifice, God welcomes you into relationship with him with open arms.

Paul put it this way: *"He forgave us all our sins, having canceled the charge of our legal indebtedness, which stood against us and condemned us; he has taken it away, nailing it to the cross"* (Colossians 2:13, 14).

Live it

God took away your 'list' of sins. He nailed it to the cross. He is never going to bring it up again. Maybe it's time for you to put your list away and thank God for the forgiveness you have in Jesus Christ.

Day 24

Hear it

Well then, should we keep on sinning so that God can show us more and more of his wonderful grace? Of course not! Since we have died to sin, how can we continue to live in it? (Romans 6:1, 2 NLT).

Believe it

"Are you saying that since I am totally forgiven, I can just go out and do whatever I want to do?"

This question isn't new. The Apostle Paul was hit with it almost everywhere he traveled. It shows up wherever and whenever the gospel of God's grace is proclaimed.

The answer throughout church history has always been the answer Paul gave in Romans 6:2: *"By no means! We are those who have died to sin; how can we live in it any longer?"* (Romans 6:2).

Forgiveness isn't the whole story of the Gospel. Not only did God forgive every one of our sins, he broke sin's power and control in our lives.

When we were lost, we were under the control of sin's power and held there by the law. But when we died in Christ, that power was broken once and for all. This freed us to be joined to another.

So what did God do? He raised us to walk in the newness of life led by and empowered by the Holy Spirit. You have died to sin. You now belong to Christ and *"serve in the new way of the Spirit"* (Romans 7:6).

Forgiveness is the opening chapter of the Gospel story. It is not a chapter that leads us back to our old way of life. It's a chapter that builds the foundation of God's grace into our lives and leads us forward to walking in the newness of life.

As believers in Christ, we are free to go back...to submit to the desires of the flesh or the temptations of the world. But that's not who we are anymore. We are new through and through and liberated to follow the lead of God's Spirit.

This is the door forgiveness opens for each of us. It's the door to experiencing the life of Jesus Christ by grace through faith. It's the door that leads to a life marked by love, joy, peace, patience, kindness, goodness, faithfulness, gentleness and self-control.

No, total forgiveness of sins does not lead to reckless living. On the contrary, this gift of grace connects us to the love of Jesus Christ and compels us to a life of faith in him..."*dead to sin, but alive to God in Christ Jesus*" (Romans 6:11).

Live it

In Christ, you've died to sin and have been raised to walk in the newness of life. Forgiveness of sins opened the door for you to experience life to the full. Walk through and enjoy your new life in Christ.

Day 25

Hear it

...as far as the east is from the west, so far has he removed our transgressions from us (Psalm 103:12).

Believe it

Would it surprise you to know that in 1 Corinthians 7:11-13 the word translated *"divorce"* (some translations render the word, *"put away"*) is the Greek word for forgiveness?

Paul strongly counsels against divorce for Christian men. They are not to send their wives away.

But that is exactly what God did with your sins. He sent them away.

In essence, Jesus *"divorced"* you from your sins and sent them away forever.

The Day of Atonement foreshadowed this truth. On that day, the high priest took two male goats and cast lots to determine the goat to sacrifice and the goat to send out in the wilderness. This second goat is known as the scapegoat.

After the blood was sprinkled on the mercy seat, the high priest would present the live goat. He ceremoniously transferred the sins of the people to the head of the goat. And then the goat was sent away into the wilderness, carrying away the sins of the people.

This scapegoat was symbolic of the real forgiveness we receive in Christ.

In forgiving you, God sent your sins away. Where are they? *"As far as the east is from the west"*—an infinite distance away.

Live it

God divorced you from your sins. He removed them. He sent them away. He remembers them no more. This is forgiveness. This is grace.

Day 26

Hear it

There is no fear in love. But perfect love drives out fear, because fear has to do with punishment. The one who fears is not made perfect in love (1 John 4:18).

Believe it

Fear has been part of the human story since the Garden. After Adam and Eve chose to eat of the tree of the knowledge of good and evil, fear took control of their lives. It became a part of their spiritual DNA.

Notice how Adam responded when God called out to him after his catastrophic decision: *"I heard you in the garden, and I was afraid because I was naked; so I hid"* (Genesis 3:10). This is what raw fear looks like.

Tragically, Adam and Eve passed this fear on to you. You came into the world with fear in your heart. And specifically, as John wrote, this fear you inherited "has to do with punishment."

We know deep down our sins deserve to be punished. But when and how? That's what we fear. This is why so many people think the bad circumstances life throws their way are really God's way of punishing them for some sin they committed.

This underlying fear is devastating whenever we mess up. It causes us to wonder, "How could God love me?" But none of that does anything about the fear.

There is only one way to drive this fear away. It is the perfect love of God. The love of God that nailed your sins to a cross. The love of God that sent them away once and for all. The love of God that remembers your sins no more.

God demonstrated this love for you at the cross. *"In this is love, not that we have loved God but he loved us and sent his Son to be the propitiation for our sins"* (1 John 4:10 ESV).

There is no need to worry about punishment. Jesus took all of it on the cross. This was the love of God in action. It has been poured out into your heart. Walk in it. It will drive the fear away.

God loves you, and the grace he lavished on you to provide redemption, the forgiveness of sins, is the proof.

Live it

Don't let fear and shame dictate your relationship with God. The thing you fear has been handled. Jesus gladly paid the penalty for your sins. You don't need to hide from God, or try to appease him to turn aside punishment.

No, you can approach God with full confidence knowing that nothing can separate you from his love, not even your sins.

Day 27

Hear it

I am writing to you, dear children, because your sins have been forgiven on account of his name (I John 2:12).

Believe it

Many believers are stuck in the past. They often say, *"I know God has forgiven me, but I am having a hard time forgiving myself."*

Have you heard people you know say this? Maybe it's something you are struggling with right now. If so, you are not alone. Many people find it difficult to forgive themselves.

There is not a verse or a passage in the Bible that teaches self-forgiveness. Jesus never said to anyone that they need to forgive themselves.

Here is the reason. All sins are ultimately against God. We are in his debt, not our own. It is his choice to forgive or not to forgive. The good news is this – He chose to forgive all of our sins in Christ. That's grace.

Forgiveness means that you and I have been released from the punishment our sins deserved. Jesus stood in our place. He bore our sins in his body. He paid the penalty for sin. As Paul wrote, *"the wages of sin is death"* (Romans 6:23). Jesus died for you and me.

Instead of holding on to the past, maybe it's time to apply God's forgiveness to our lives. Maybe it's time to let go of the guilt, the shame and the condemnation. Maybe it's time to fully believe John's message to the children of God: *"your sins have been forgiven on account of his name"* (1 John 2:12).

Live it

God, in his authority and power, forgave you through the shed blood of Jesus Christ. As C. S. Lewis so eloquently stated, *"I think that if God forgives us we must forgive ourselves."*

Open your heart and let his forgiveness pour in and free you from your past. Let his grace rip away the guilt and shame. Let his love set you on the path of genuinely living out who you are in Jesus Christ.

Day 28

Hear it

Be kind and compassionate to one another, forgiving each other, just as in Christ God forgave you (Ephesians 4:32).

Believe it

If God is the only one who has the authority and power to forgive sins, why does the Bible encourage us to forgive others? That is a good question to think through.

In forgiving our sins, God did much more than speak forgiveness into our lives. He sent Jesus to die in our place, to shed his blood for our sins. That was a must. The Bible is clear. *"Without the shedding of blood, there is no forgiveness of sins"* (Hebrews 9:22).

In that sacrifice, he removed our sins, placed them on himself, suffered the punishment for them, sent them away, and then chose to remember them no more. How can we do that?

Even if we died for someone else, would our blood be sufficient to take that person's sin away? The answer is a resounding no. We can't do for another person what Jesus Christ did for us.

We can, however, extend grace to another person based on the shed blood of Jesus. This is the nature of Paul's encouragement to the believers in Ephesus and Colossae and to us.

In his letter to the Ephesians, Paul wrote, *"Be kind and compassionate to one another, forgiving each other, just as in Christ God forgave you"* (Ephesians 4:32). To the Colossians he wrote, *"Bear with each other and forgive one another if any of you has a grievance against someone. Forgive as the Lord forgave you"* (Colossians 3:13).

In both of these verses, Paul uses the word *charizomai*. The root word is *charis*, which means "grace." In this context, to forgive is to willingly extend kindness and favor to another person. To forgive as the Lord forgave you is an extension of God's grace to you

Live it

Is there someone who has offended or wronged you? On the basis of Christ's shed blood, reach out to that person and extend the kindness of the Lord, seventy times seven. You'll be glad you did, for their benefit and for yours.

Day 29

Hear it

Therefore, there is now no condemnation for those who are in Christ Jesus (Romans 8:1).

Believe it

Joe showed up every Tuesday. The Bible Study was important to him. He came because his marriage was falling apart. His wife was fed up and wanted a divorce. Joe was doing his best to hold on as tightly as he could.

Everything he tried widened the gap between them, moving them further and further apart. As his relationship continued to spiral out of control, all hope for the marriage started to vanish.

At the heart of Joe's problem was his confusion as to how God viewed all of this, and specifically how God would view him if his marriage ended in divorce. In his mind, Joe believed God's anger toward him grew by the minute.

But he continued to show up every Tuesday hoping to find that one nugget of truth that would change his wife's mind and convince her to stay in the marriage.

I tried to shift his thinking. *"Joe,"* I said, *"when you come to Bible study, open your heart to the message God has for you."*

Two years passed. One night after the study, Joe grabbed me to talk. He looked different. He asked me, *"Have you guys been teaching this stuff all along?"*

"What stuff, Joe?"

"Forgiveness—that Christ has totally forgiven all of my sins."

I couldn't believe what I was hearing. Forgiveness was front and center every single week. The message was being delivered, but Joe wasn't hearing it.

He was so concerned about saving his marriage, and keeping God from being angry at him that he completely missed the message God had for him.

That night, the truth broke through to Joe and his eyes were opened. Joe could finally see beyond God's justice into God's heart of love for him. This changed everything for Joe and for his marriage.

Operating from an attitude of fear wasn't helping Joe or the marriage at all. He needed to believe the truth and stand on the foundation that in Christ, there is no condemnation.

Live it

What if you actually believed that God forgave all of your sins in Christ? What if you took your stand on the truth that in Christ there is no condemnation? What if you lived each day knowing that nothing can separate you from the love of God? What if you trusted the love of God to guide you through the trials and tribulations of life?

Here is the good news. The forgiveness of God and love of God are not "what ifs." Your sins have been forgiven. There is no condemnation for you in Christ. This is true of you.

Day 30

Hear it

All this is from God, who reconciled us to himself through Christ and gave us the ministry of reconciliation: that God was reconciling the world to himself in Christ, not counting people's sins against them. And he has committed to us the message of reconciliation (2 Corinthians 5:18, 19).

Believe it

"All of this is from God."

God took the initiative. He reconciled you to himself in Christ.

There is nothing more that needs to be done. The barrier that stood between you and God is gone.

At a point in your life, this message, the good news, found its way to your heart. You believed it and were reconciled to God.

Paul put it this way in his letter to the Romans: *"More than that, we also rejoice in God through our Lord Jesus Christ, through whom we have now received reconciliation"* (Romans 5:11 *ESV*).

Now here is what *"all of this"* means to you.

Forgiveness is yours.

All that fear and hostility you held toward God are gone.

You are no longer at odds with him.

Now you and God are in harmony with one another…on the same page… brought into friendship with him.

You are free to enjoy a dynamic and vibrant relationship with Jesus.

All because his work on the cross did a work in your heart. Remember this truth.

Live it

The world will try to keep the narrative that God is mad at you alive in your mind. It will continually tell you that you are at odds with Him. It's not true.

Cast it aside. You have been reconciled to God. Your sins have been forgiven. You are in relationship with the One who loved you and gave Himself for you.

Live it to the full by grace, through faith. There is nothing holding you back.

Dear Reader,

I pray that this devotional has deepened your understanding of Jesus' finished work on the cross. Forgiveness is yours. You can rest in the fact that nothing can separate you from his love. May your heart respond in thankfulness.

I would love to stay in contact with you. Please feel free to reach out to me at bob@basicgospel.net I also invite you to join me each weekday for *Basic Gospel*, either on your local station (basicgospel.net/stations) or at Facebook.com/basicgospel
or YouTube.com/basicgospel.

In Him,

Bob Christopher
@rcchristopherjr

Scan the QR code for quick access.

"We're all natural-born legalists," says Bob Christopher. "We try to live for God, but it's impossible to do."

Why? Because all our efforts and ideas are based on the same fear-based, guilt-driven plot line: Try harder. As you've undoubtedly noticed, it just doesn't work.

Simple Gospel, Simply Grace showcases an alternative, which is actually God's original plan: Everything you're trying to achieve in the Christian life has already been given to you—from God, by grace, in Christ.

Do you struggle to receive what God has freely given? How can you begin to experience true freedom, assurance of your forgiveness, and victory over sin? How can the power that raised Jesus from the dead enable you to live and love the way He did?

You'll discover the answers in this crystal-clear portrayal of the simple gospel—which is simply grace.

Get your copy today!
simplegospelsimplygrace.com
or 844.412.2742

Simple Gospel

How Your Christian Life is Really Supposed to Work

Simply Grace

Bob Christopher

www.ingramcontent.com/pod-product-compliance
Lightning Source LLC
Chambersburg PA
CBHW051045030426
42339CB00006B/215

9 7 8 1 9 3 1 8 9 9 4 5 1